Thoughts on Happiness
Rashik Parmar

Copyright © 2017 Rashik Parmar.

All rights reserved. No part of this book may be reproduced, stored, or transmitted by any means—whether auditory, graphic, mechanical, or electronic—without written permission of the author, except in the case of brief excerpts used in critical articles and reviews. Unauthorized reproduction of any part of this work is illegal and is punishable by law.

This book is a work of non-fiction. Unless otherwise noted, the author and the publisher make no explicit guarantees as to the accuracy of the information contained in this book and in some cases, names of people and places have been altered to protect their privacy.

ISBN: 978-1-4834-7277-5 (sc)
ISBN: 978-1-4834-7278-2 (e)

Because of the dynamic nature of the Internet, any web addresses or links contained in this book may have changed since publication and may no longer be valid. The views expressed in this work are solely those of the author and do not necessarily reflect the views of the publisher, and the publisher hereby disclaims any responsibility for them.

Any people depicted in stock imagery provided by Thinkstock are models, and such images are being used for illustrative purposes only. Certain stock imagery © Thinkstock.

Lulu Publishing Services rev. date: 11/3/2017

Background

At the start of 2016, I challenged myself to write a Facebook status message related to happiness every week. Everyone wants happiness and yet it is difficult to describe or understand. We all do things that we hope will create happiness for ourselves or others. However, the result is far from what we expected. Observing a general decline in the happiness of people around me, I felt I needed to do something. At the time, it seemed like a nice idea and a well-intentioned new year's resolution. Little did I know how difficult this was going to be and the effort required to create simple whilst poignant weekly messages on happiness.

I did persist and am pleased to say that I wrote 53 thoughts on happiness in 2016. The feedback I received from friends and family suggested that these thoughts would be valuable for others and so decide to embark on producing this short book. To make the book more engaging, each thought is accompanied by a picture that was taken by myself. Each picture has been chosen to capture the thought and I hope makes the book more interesting.

I have many to thank for encouraging and supporting me in writing this book. None more so that my wife for being patient and supportive in this quest. Many of her Sunday mornings were disturbed with discussions on these thoughts and there is a lot of her perspectives in each thought. Also, my two children who encouraged me to complete this quest in understanding happiness.

My hope is that these thoughts will play a part in helping you increase the happiness in your life.

Week 1

As we start the new year, consider being thankful for all the happiness of the past years.

Future hopes and dreams will help us find where happiness may emerge. What is your plan to turn those hopes and dreams into a reality?

Patience and persistence are often our best friends on this happiness journey.

Week 2

We need to constantly be aware of the gap between dreams and delusion.

Use your dreams to guide your actions.

Use the results from those actions to understand your capabilities and realise the boundary of delusion.

Week 3

Happiness is a state of mind that you can always choose.

At a moment of loss or failure, sadness and grief is the natural response. Using the happiness of special moments in the past, provides the strength and courage to come to terms with your new reality. Remember to look up and see all your friends/relatives that are there to share your future happiness. Use this to choose happiness.

Week 4

By giving a sincere gift of kindness something special happens. Not only do you improve some else's life and making them happy, you are also rewarded with happiness.

What gift of kindness could you give today?

Week 5

We all dream about future happiness, and often choose short term suffering to realise this future dream.

However, happiness is not just a destination, happiness is also a journey.

Ask yourself if there is a path that provides happiness and leads to much deeper happiness in the future.

Week 6

There seems to be four stages of happiness:

1. Unlocking the desire for happiness and realising this is choice we all have

2. Listening for and reflecting on the happiness around us and within us

3. Finding our own path of happiness

4. Achieving a state of eternal happiness

What stages have you observed?

What stage will you focus on this week?

Week 7

As we approach Valentine's day, the unconditional love between two people is wonderful to see and experience.

Is happiness the result of or reason for unconditional love?

Let's hope everyone can experience the unique glow from unconditional love.

Week 8

Is there a link between peacefulness and happiness? Being at peace with yourself and your current situation allows happiness to bubble to the surface. Just like bubbles when opening a fizzy pop bottle.

Are you at peace with yourself and your situation?

Can your happiness bubble to the surface?

Week 9

Is there a link between jealousy and happiness?

In many ways, jealousy stems from being unhappy about an aspect of yourself. You must use this feeling to better understand yourself. There is often a deep-rooted experience that is linked to the jealousy. Coming to terms with this can help unlock feelings of calm and happiness...

Week 10

Often the poorest people seem to be the happiest. Being part of a community that really cares about everyone's wellbeing is important to an individual's happiness.

Do you feel you have the community around you to be happy?

Week 11

Are mothers the primary giver of happiness or even the embodiment of happiness?

Their selfless devotion to nurturing and protecting their children is remarkable to experience. We should all be thankful for those special moments of happiness with our mother. Are you taking time to be grateful for all the happiness your mother has provided and helping her find happiness?

Week 12

How can some people can find happiness in almost any activity?

Understand why every activity matters. Be focused on that single task. Giving your all to this moment is a route to happiness right now.

Have you experienced this?

Week 13

March 20 is World Happiness Day. The latest world happiness report makes interesting reading.

Giving has been the top way to create happiness for several years.

So what do you plan to give to create happiness on March 20?

http://worldhappiness.report

Week 14

How does your environment affect your happiness?

Your environment triggers memories and emotions that can have a direct impact on your mood and happiness.

Changing environment can both allow you to help make others happy and increase your personal happiness.

Are you doing enough to create an environment for happiness to emerge?

Week 15

What can we do to appreciate what we have and help increase our happiness?

Sometimes we are so caught up in progress that we forget to appreciate what we have. This constant pursuit for progress doesn't give us time to be happy here and now. Look at all you should be happy about now.

http://www.huffingtonpost.com/paula-tursi/happiness_b_1828838.html

Week 16

Would winning the lottery really increase your happiness?

The lottery ticket is a donation to a charity with a slim chance of winning a life changing amount of money. The lottery prize can change your life, but if it is happiness that you are looking for, then you may need to look elsewhere. Investing in the happiness of others can yield a prize more valuable than a lottery prize.

Week 17

Is there a limit to happiness?

Your current situation may make you think that there are limits. However, happiness comes from understanding what matters to you and satisfying those deep desires. With the help of others, we can uncover those deep desires. Understanding what matters to us helps uncover our happiness. The deeper we go the happier we can become. So, there is no limit to happiness.

Week 18

Can you have too much happiness?

When everything is going right and you feel your happiness is at a peak, one of the risks you face is becoming arrogant. Arrogance can have a negative impact on others making them unhappy and ultimately destroys your happiness. When things are going well, ask others to judge your behaviour and watch for the signs of arrogance.

Week 19

Are happiness and faith connected?

Life seems synonymous with ups and downs, highs and lows, happiness and sadness. Being able to cope with those lows tends to take faith in a greater good. This interesting study sheds light on how faith has an impact on happiness.

http://www.today.com/kindness/study-religion-faith-can-help-provide-sustained-happiness-t39036

Week 20

Does being happy require you stay focused on the here and now?

Dwelling on past happiness leads to feelings of sadness. Dreaming of future happiness means we do not take time to appreciate everything that we should be happy about right now. Happiness can only be experienced one moment at a time. Past happiness should add fuel to the current happiness and dreams should inspire us to take the right actions at every moment. Are you making the most of every moment of happiness that you have?

Week 21

What words of wisdom ignite your happiness?

"Happiness cannot be travelled to, owned, earned, worn or consumed. Happiness is the spiritual experience of living every minute with love, grace, and gratitude." *Denis Waitley*

Check out some more happiness quotes.

http://www.inc.com/jeff-haden/75-inspiring-motivational-quotes-for-being-happier.html

Week 22

What happiness should you be thankful for?

Some people are always complaining about how things were much better in the past. The reality is that they didn't take time to be thankful for everything they had or have.

Take a moment to list all the things you should be thankful for now and experience how your happiness grows.

Week 23

Do you need to be able to clear your mind to find happiness?

There are times when our mind is full of all the things that we need to do, had promised to do, felt we should do and so on... This kind of cluttered mind hides the weak happiness signals. Eknath Easwaran provides simple and clear guidance on how to clear the mind and fully release the hidden happiness...

http://yameditation.org/blog/2016/5/31/eknath-easwaran-an-uncluttered-mind

Week 24

Life is full of tests, are you ready?

As we start the examination season, stress levels seem to be high in children and parents. This stress seems to mask the inner happiness and create strained relationships. However, their life so far has been preparing them for these tests. Remember happiness awaits as the next stage of life begins.

Week 25

Do what you really care about and you will get the best rewards...

Happiness can be a result of an achievement that is beyond our imagination. Doing the things that we really care about without any expectation of reward or recognition allows us to focus on being our best and achieve things that cannot be imagined. This is referred to as Nishkan Bhakti within the Hindu beliefs. Something that we should all learn as this encourages selfless actions that unlock sincere inner happiness and rewards you cannot imagine.

http://www.spiritualawareness.co.in/spirituality/bhakti-yog.aspx

Week 26

How has your father helped you find happiness?

Fathers come in many sizes and shapes. However, they all seem to have something in common. They inspire us to be our best, unlock that courage that is often masked by fear. Encourage us to try a little harder, reach a little further, and find that extra reserve of energy. They are always waiting patiently to congratulate us and share in our happiness. Take a moment to thank your Father for helping you find your happiness helping make you who you are.

Happy Father's day.

Week 27

Does happiness emerge from hope?

The anxiety and fear that comes from uncertainty often results in unhappiness. This is a time when the right leaders are able provide hope of a better future through a vision that unifies. Leaders need to inspire the right actions that allow the vision to become a reality. At a moment of uncertainty find the hope of a better future and happiness will remerge.

Week 28

Is isolation the antithesis of happiness?

Being alone for a short period can provide time for reflection and renewal. However, prolonged periods of isolation seem to lead to deep depression. Just a two-minute phone call can transform someone's perspective and make them feel loved again. Naturally leading back to a state of happiness. So, if you know someone that is living alone, how about making contact? Take them some biscuits. That day you will walk with a spring in your step, because your inner happiness will rocket up. Go on make a lonely person feel happy today.

Week 29

How happy are you?

You cannot see what you look like without using an aid, such as a mirror. In the same way, it is very difficult to know how happy you are without a tool. There is a useful tool to measure your happiness level - Thanks to Sushila Issar for sharing this tool...

http://www.chopra.com/ccl/where-do-you-stack-up-on-the-happiness-scale

Week 30

Can random acts of kindness multiply happiness?

Random acts of kindness can be a great way to help increase the happiness in the world. Just like the ripples created from a drop of water of falling into a still lake. This kindness will create ripples of kindness resulting in waves of happiness...

What random act of kindness will you use to help increase the happiness in the world today?

Week 31

Is having a loving spouse essential for happiness?

There are certain memories that fuel inner happiness in a manner that you cannot stop yourself from wearing a massive smile. The loving care and support from a spouse helps us achieve goals previously unimaginable. Hoping that everyone can find their special partner that brings them that special happiness only possible through marriage.

Remember to thank your spouse for being so special.

Week 32

Is summer the season of happiness?

The scent from the flowers seems to ignite our inner happiness. The sun (when it comes out in the UK!) seems to make everyone happier somehow. Is there something we can do to make this happiness last into the winter months or is it that we must experience winter to fully appreciate the summer happiness?

Week 33

Can babies teach us how to be happy?

Some babies seem to be born to be happy and seem to create happiness in everyone they meet. I watched a family with a happy baby in a train recently and the happiness this baby emanated seemed to fill the whole train coach. I wonder how we could also learn the secret to become the source of happiness wherever we go?

Week 34

Can religious festivals like the Hindu festival of Raksha Bandan create happiness?

Sisters will tie a Rakhi around their brother's wrists. A sign of their prayers for their brother's wellbeing. There are many historical and mythological stories about how this tradition began. This and many similar festivals fuel the happiness in families. Both brother and sister being reminded they are connected from birth and knowing they will support each other create an inner happiness...

Week 35

Is feeling happy the same as being happy?

I wonder if people sometimes confuse feeling happy with being happy. Instant gratification from the digitally connected world seems to make this the norm. Happiness from material acquisitions can make us forget about the deeper desire to be happy. Take a moment to ask yourself what being happy means to you and commit to one small action that you could do now to make a step towards being happy.

Week 36

Are anger and happiness connected?

Anger is often used to overcome an obstacle to achieving happiness and can be an effective tool, if used sparingly. However, it can leave resentment with everyone involved and leave an enduring corrosive impact on an individual's happiness. Finding a way to recognise this resentment exists and coming to terms with the situation is vital to increase happiness.

How can you do that?

Discussing your feeling with a friend over a warm beverage followed by a favourite form of introspection or mindfulness can be effective.

Is resentment from past anger holding back your happiness

Week 37

Is advertising limiting your happiness?

By following images that you see in advertisements, bill boards, and other media we are encouraged to become like those images. We forget to understand ourselves. What matters for us and why? What does happiness mean for us? Only if we can find this inner peace can we make significant steps on the journey to happiness.

https://www.sharecare.com/health/happiness/how-self-aware-make-happy

Week 38

Does being disconnected lead to unhappiness?

Social contact is a fundamental need for all humans. Reading about those that become isolated for a range of reasons there seems to be a common coping strategy. They used the happiness from past contacts to cope with their suffering. Whilst mobile technologies can help here, there is no substitute for meeting in person. What can we all do to help connect with those that are being isolated from society around us?

A BFG dream jar...

Placed around London

2016...

![BFG dream jar photograph]

https://invitation2events.wordpress.com/2016/07/16/the-bfg-dream-jar-trail/

Week 39

Is happiness only a dream away?

Childhood stories seem to be filled with hope that the magic fairy or giant is going to magically solve all our problems and destroy the evil that is the cause of all our sadness. Should we all learn from these stories and start to dream of a happier world that will encourage us to make that a reality...

Week 40

Are you making the right choices to create happiness for yourselves and those around you?

We all have a choice of how to respond to any situation and in this choice, hides the opportunity of happiness. You in the form of your actions are the root of your happiness.

"Between stimulus and response there is a space. In that space is our power to choose our response. In our response lies our growth and our freedom."

– Victor Frankl

Week 41

Is there a link between dance and happiness?

Scientific research has shown there is a strong linkage.

So, next time you are feeling a little down, why not consider playing some uplifting music and having a little dance with loved one.

http://www.happify.com/hd/the-science-of-happy/ .

Week 42

Do we have to learn forgiveness to increase the happiness for ourselves and others?

Tragic situations are sometimes the ones that bring out the true meaning of happiness. Simon Kennedy whose mother died on 9/11 lives with that reality every day of his life. His message of forgiveness and tolerance is one that leads to happiness. We can all learn from his story.

http://hope1032.com.au/stories/life/inspirational-stories/2014/911-and-the-art-of-happiness/

Week 43

Is caring the secret to making someone's birthday a happy one?

We often wish friends and relatives a happy birthday, but to make that day special requires attention to detail. Understanding what the individual likes and dislikes, not as a gift but activities, food, location and conversation. So, like most things in life caring is at the centre of creating happiness.

Week 44

Are we making the most of the happiness we have?

Dwelling on what could or should have been creates sadness. Phrases like "I should have got that job", "that customer did not understand what we could really offer" or simply "it's not fair" as one upset child shouts to her mother.

How can we help people learn from these situations? One approach is to discuss the actions that led to this situation and identify the ways things could have been different. Realising the outcome can be affected by our actions and that there are many things to be happy about right now allows us to come to terms with the reality and get back to enjoying the current happiness.

Week 45

Is there a special happiness when a loved one returns?

The Hindu festival of Diwali (Festival of lights) to mark the return of Ram from the forest after killing the demon Ravan. Ram was exiled to the forest for 14 years and there is a chance that he might have forgotten his way home. Diwa (lanterns) are placed in windows and doorways to guide Ram's path. The happiness that is evident when the brothers meet reminds us of the true essence of happiness that is hidden in loving relationships.

Why not meet or get in contact with an old friend or distant relative, to bring happiness to them as well as yourself today.

Week 46

Does forgiveness open the path to happiness?

There is a strong connection between adversity and happiness. Terry Waite's story is a good illustration of this. During his 5 years in solitary confinement and captivity, he had suffered in ways that we cannot imagine. In this quote, he reminds us that the path to happiness lies in forgiveness.

"If one can understand why people behave as they do then often the road to forgiveness is opened. Not only is forgiveness essential for the health of Society, it is also vital for our personal well-being. Bitterness is like a cancer that enters the soul. It does more harm to those that hold it than to those whom it is held against." – Terry Waite

Week 47

Is there happiness in losing?

The sorrow and misery that we can observe on an athlete's face as they don't win a medal may lead you to think there is only happiness in winning. However, we forget all the smaller wins that brought them to the competition. The skills and expertise that came out of the hours of practice will enable future successes. Thinking of happiness as a journey with each loss as paving the way to future happiness allows us to share in the happiness of the winners.

Week 48

Do we confuse possession of nice things and happiness?

People say that they will be happy if they can buy a new house or own a luxury car. However, those that have these possessions don't seem to be happy and look for other possessions, fitness, weight loss or health. Those that are truly grateful for all they have seem to be happy all the time. So maybe we should focus on appreciating what we have, to find our happiness.

Week 49

Are the optimists the only ones that are happy?

The pessimists seen to be able to always find something that could be better. Something to complain about or find the risks in a plan. Yet they too can find things that make them happy. Things to laugh at.

Maybe the pessimists help everyone see the things they should be grateful for and so find their happiness. Take a moment today to find those that have helped you find happiness and say thank you.

Week 50

Can there be happiness without sadness?

Do we need sadness and suffering to appreciate happiness? That may be why a poor person can be happy with all the things they have, while the rich person can be unhappy thinking about all the things they do not have.

Week 51

Are happiness and freedom connected?

Giving someone freedom can create happiness just as taking someone's freedom away can create unhappiness. Historical stories of slavery are very good examples. However, like with most things in life there are boundaries. One person's freedom can become another person's punishment.

Freedom of speech means that we can say things that are so hurtful that they can destroy relationships for a lifetime. So, we all need to learn to respect and cherish freedom for all in a manner that allows everyone's happiness to flourish.

Week 52

Is happiness real?

Our senses help us experience the world. The brain is the place where our version of reality exists. This leads us to think that happiness is also experienced in the brain. However, there are times when we just feel happy for no reason at all and other times we feel down. Is something deeper that is the inner source of happiness. Is it from that life-giving spirit that we call the soul that happiness emanates? As the soul is the essence of I, is being able to truly get connected with the soul the path to real happiness for an individual?

Week 53

Is the gift of love the pathway to happiness?

We tend to focus on giving material gifts many of which will be put into cupboards and forgotten. However, the gift that can be both free and priceless at the same time, is the gift of love. Take a moment to think about how you can show your love to someone dear to you and help them unlock some happiness in their life.